THIS JOURNAL BELONGS TO

SHINE BRIGHT

PRODUCTIVITY JOURNAL

CHRONICLE BOOKS
SAN FRANCISCO

PAGE NO.	TABLE OF CONTENTS

PAGE NO.	TABLE OF CONTENTS

PAGE NO.	TABLE OF CONTENTS

PAGE NO.	TABLE OF CONTENTS

PAGE NO.	TABLE OF CONTENTS

PAGE NO.	TABLE OF CONTENTS